A Teach Me About Book

I Love Grandma and Grandpa

A Teach Me About Book

I Love Grandma and Grandpa

Joy Berry

A long time ago, my mommy and daddy were little, just like me.

When my mommy was little, she had a mommy and daddy.

When my daddy was little, he had a mommy and daddy.

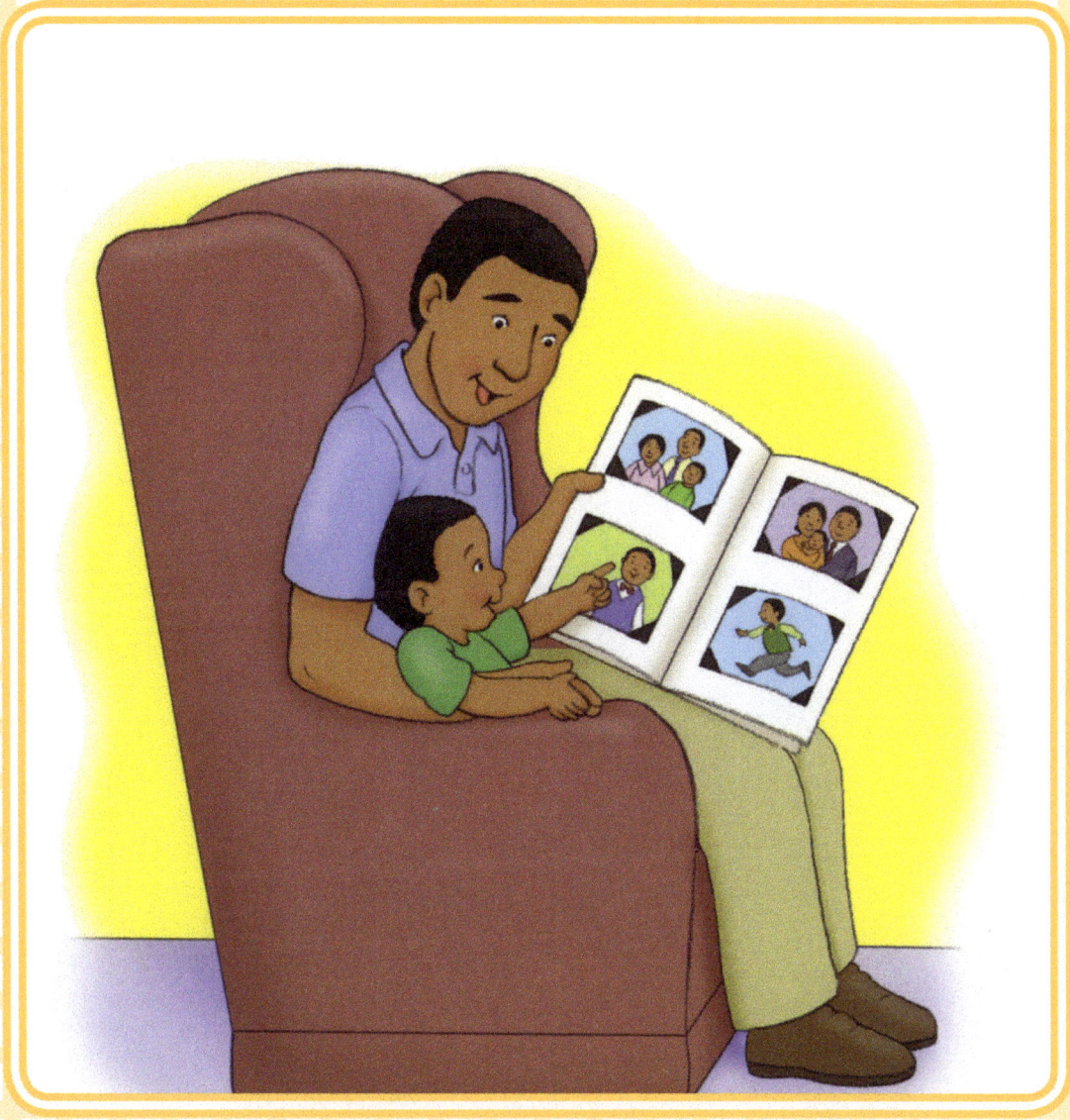

My daddy grew up.

His mommy grew older and became my grandma.

His daddy grew older and became my grandpa.

My mommy grew up.

Her mommy grew older and became my grandma.

Her daddy grew older and became my grandpa.

Sometimes when I am with my grandma and grandpa we do things together.

Sometimes when I am with my grandma and grandpa, I do things by myself.

I try to be good when I am with my grandma and grandpa.

I do what they ask me to do without complaining.

I try to be good when I am with my grandma and grandpa.

I do not do things they do not want me to do.

I try to be good when I am with my grandma and grandpa.

I help them as much as I can.

I love my grandma and grandpa!

When we cannot be together, we send things to each other.

We talk to each other on the telephone.

We look forward to the time when we can be together again.

CPSIA information can be obtained
at www.ICGtesting.com
Printed in the USA
LVHW072143050919
630145LV00014B/294/P

9 780739 602874